D1833084

A HORSE BOOK

BY

MARY TOURTEL

©Reserved

All rights reserved. No part of this work may be reproduced, stored, adapted, or transmitted in any form or by any means, electronic, mechanical, photocopying, micro-filming recording or otherwise, or translated in any language, without the prior written permission of the copyright owner and the publisher. The book is sold subject to the condition that it shall not, by way of trade or otherwise, be lent, resold, hired out, or otherwise circulated without the prior publisher's written consent in any form of binding or cover other than that in which it is published.

The views and opinions expressed in this book are author(s) own and the facts reported by them have been verified to the extent possible, and the publishers are not in any way liable for the same.

First Published in 1901
Indian Reprint in 2017

Published by

Kalpaz Publications
C-30, Satyawati Nagar,
Delhi – 110052
E-mail: kalpaz@hotmail.com
Website: kalpazpublications.com
Ph.: +91-9212142040

Cataloging in Publication Data—DK
Courtesy: D.K. Agencies (P) Ltd. <docinfo@dkagencies.com>

Tourtel, Mary, author.
A horse book / by Mary Tourtel.
pages cm
"First published in 1901"—Title page verso.
ISBN 9789351284253 (HB)

1. Horses—Juvenile poetry. 2. Horses—Juvenile literature.
3. Children's poetry, English. I. Title.

LCC PZ10.3.T68Hor 2017 | DDC 821.9 23

CONTENTS.

M.T.

AT PLAY.

THREE little foals you see at
play.
They romp and sport all through
the day,
But sometimes they are most
sedate
And try to ape their mothers'
gait.

They wheel and race and leap
and prance,
And sometimes they are said
to dance :
But always they will stand and
stare
At anyone who passes there.

SCHOOLING.

THE horse, like us, must go to
 school
To learn by precept and by
 rule.
Like us, he does not love the
 work,
Like us, he's not allowed to
 shirk.

This little instrument you see
Strapped on his back, shaped
 like a V,
Is a "Dumb Jockey" meant to
 train
The horse to bear the bit and
 rein.

M.T

P FOR PONY
A FOR APPLE
C FOR CLOWN
D FOR DUNCE
B FOR BOY
M.T.

CLEVERNESS.

BILLY, the circus pony, can
Distinguish letters like a man:
He'll hold up for you in the
ring
His D for Dunce and K for
King.

With P for Pony he will show
That he his family name doth
know;
And he will find the C for
clown
And at his feet will put it
down.

WILLINGNESS.

ALTHOUGH this horse is doing all he can to drag his heavy load up the hill, the lazy boy who is walking beside him, with one hand in his pocket, beats him cruelly with the stick which he carries. The boy is too silly or too careless to see how willingly the horse is working.

M.T.

WILFULNESS.

A HORSE's great red-letter days
Are days of hunting, when his
ways
Are often very wilful. Here
See this John Gilpin in great
fear.

He came out just to see the
Meet,
But the horse thought he would
compete
With horses, hounds and fox
for place,
And led the man this madcap
race.

INTELLIGENCE.

On the prairies in the Far West of America a man lost his way. He had no water to drink, although both he and his horse were parched with thirst. Not knowing where to find water, he cast the reins on the neck of his horse. By means of that wonderful intelligence which some people wrongly call instinct, the horse found his way to a spring, although it was many miles distant. Thus both man and horse were able to quench their thirst, and in this way their lives were saved.

M.T.

KICKING.

THESE two are very much dis-
mayed
To see the fuss their horse has
made
Because this dog in playful
mood
Barked in a manner rather
rude.

It is a thing some horses do
Until the driver makes them
rue
Their fits of temper. Then
they say
That kicking doesn't seem to
pay.

GENTLENESS.

THESE big carthorses and these little children are great friends. Although the horses are so big, they are very gentle, and allow the carter's children to lead them home in the evening, or to ride on their backs.

BITING.

PEGGY is the children's pride,
And she allows them all to ride.
She comes to them whene'er
they call,
And loves to have them in her
stall.

With others she has wilful
ways.
She will be cross with John for
days,
Will kick and squeal, will show
much spite,
And very often try to bite.

TOILING.

THESE three horses are ploughing an upland field. They are thoroughly enjoying themselves, for they are so strong that their work is a pleasure to them. The ploughman is guiding the plough, so as to keep the furrows straight. The rooks are soaring round in search of grubs found in the earth which is turned up by the plough.

M.T.

M.T.

HUNTING.

WHAT sweeter sound on winter
morn
Than music of the hounds and
horn?
What prettier sight could e'er
be seen
Than hounds and horses on the
green?

See winding down this country
way
An eager throng one winter
day.
Keen are the men for sport of
course,
But just as keen each hound
and horse.

DUTY.

THE troop-horse, like all soldiers, has to learn his drill till he becomes as efficient as his rider. In war he will take his place in his squadron should his rider have been killed or wounded. In one instance, several guns of the Royal Horse Artillery were saved by the teams galloping back to their lines after all the gunners and drivers had been shot down.

M.T.

M.T.

REARING.

REARING is an awkward vice,
No rider ever thinks it nice.
When the horse prances on two
feet
It's difficult to keep one's seat.

This lady riding in the Row
Is a good rider, you must know.
When on two legs her horse
would soar
She quickly brings him down
to four.

SAGACITY.

THERE is danger at this place which the horse can see, but which the rider fails to detect. They are in the midst of a swamp where one false step would mean a horrible death in the quagmire on the verge of which the horse has pulled up. The man uses whip and spur, but the horse refuses to move. Finally the rider leaves the horse to himself to find a way round which brings them both to safety.

M T

M.T.

BOLTING.

SEE this runaway flecked with
  foam
Galloping fast as he can for
  home,
Caring nought for the shouting
  man
Running also as fast as he can.

Flung by the bolter on the
  roadside
Small is his chance of a plea-
  sant ride.
Two legs matched in a race
  with four—
Perhaps they'll meet at the
  stable door.

PATIENCE.

THE cab horse is a useful steed,
Ever handy, good at need—
A patient uncomplaining jade,
What should we do without his
  aid?

By day, by night he may be
  had,
Be the weather good or be it
  bad.
Many a knock and many a fall
He gets, and yet survives them
  all.

M.T.

M.T.

BUCKING.

WHEN horses buck they take a bound
With all their four feet off the ground.
Unless they know just what to do
And how to keep their seats all through

The riders come off fast and thick
When horses start this Yankee trick.
But with the cowboys of the West
The horses come off second best.

PERSEVERANCE.

THE horse affords the best example amongst animals of perseverance: he will go on until he falls exhausted or dead. On the Yorkshire moors, after a heavy fall of snow, the roads are quite lost, and it often happens that the mailman has to unharness his horse (the cart being blocked by the snow), and trust to the horse's courage and endurance to carry the mails from village to village. It has been known that the driver has been overcome by the intense cold, when the horse has found his way unaided to the nearest accustomed stopping place.

M. T

JIBBING.

Of all the tiresome steeds that
are
The jibber is the worst by far.
He stands and contemplates the
scene—
An act embarrassing and mean.

And nine times out of ten he
chooses
An awkward spot when he
refuses
To move. To cure him, take
him out
And turn the jibber round
about.

SERVICE.

THE Bus horse does not work
all day,
For if he did he'd waste away.
He does his work and then is
able
To take a long rest in the
stable.

When summer suns beat down
upon it
His head is sheltered by a
bonnet;
And though it makes him look
a duffer,
He hasn't half the heat to
suffer.

M.T.

SHYING.

'A WICKED horse," perhaps you
say,
"To shy in such a sudden way,
And almost make his rider fall.
It is not nice of him at all."

It was not wickedness, but fear.
That dreadful white thing rush-
ing near
Appeared to his affrighted eyes
Full seven times its proper size.

CURIOSITY.

ALL horses very curious are
And things which they espy
afar
Arouse their curiosity:
They wonder what on earth
they see.

With ears pricked up and cau-
tious mien
They come to see. When they
have seen,
They snort and turn and off
they scurry
In a contemptuous desperate
hurry.

M.T.

M.T.

FRIENDSHIP.

A BEAUTIFUL racehorse became very much attached to a cat. So much so that he was never happy unless the cat was near him, either sleeping curled up on his back or somewhere in his stall. They became such close companions that when the horse was taken abroad to run in some races for which he had been entered, he became so dejected at being separated from his companion that it was found necessary that the cat should always accompany him in his horse-box wherever he went.

OLD AGE.

THIS horse's working days are
o'er.
The shafts and saddle never-
more
Shall hold him. Here he waits
his end
Cared for by those who love to
tend

An old companion. He may
rest
In his loose box or take the
best
Of grazing which the meadows
give—
A pensioner while he shall live.

M.T.